FIGHTER PLANES

by Jeffrey Zuehlke

Lerner Publications Company • Minneapolis

For Wiley, the supersonic dog

Lerner Publications Company
A division of Lerner Publishing Group
241 First Avenue North
Minneapolis, MN 55401 U.S.A.

Website address: www.lernerbooks.com

Library of Congress Cataloging-in-Publication Data

Zuehlke, Jeffrey, 1968–
    Fighter planes / by Jeffrey Zuehlke.
        p. cm. – (Pull ahead books)
    Includes index.
    ISBN-13: 978-0-8225-2667-4 (lib. bdg. : alk. paper)
    ISBN-10: 0-8225-2667-0 (lib. bdg. : alk. paper)
    1. Fighter planes—United States—Juvenile literature. I.
Title. II. Series.
    UG1242.F5Z84 2006
    623.74'64'0973—dc22   2005007476

Manufactured in the United States of America
1 2 3 4 5 6 – JR – 11 10 09 08 07 06

Whoosh! What's that up in the sky?

It's a fighter plane! There are many kinds of fighter planes. All are fast fighting machines.

F-15 Eagles can fly 1,800 miles per hour! *F* stands for "fighter." Fighters fight enemy planes.

A-10 Thunderbolts are attack planes.
They aim at places on the ground.
The *A* stands for "attack."

F/A-18 Hornets
do two jobs.
The Hornet is a
fighter and an
attack plane.

F-16 Fighting Falcons fly high and fast.
Falcons carry powerful weapons.

F-117 Nighthawks fly at night. The Nighthawk's special shape makes it hard to find in the sky.

F/A-22 Raptors also have a special shape. The Raptor is hard to find too. It is fast and powerful.

Who flies
fighter jets?
Pilots do!

The pilot sits in the **cockpit**. Look at all the levers and buttons! They help the pilot control the plane.

The **canopy** covers the cockpit. The canopy keeps the pilot safe.

All fighter planes have wings. F-14 Tomcats can move their wings. They can stretch them out straight.

They can also
pull them back.

Big **jet engines** power fighter planes.
Engines push the plane through the sky.

Fighter planes roll on wheels. The
wheels are called landing gear.

Ready to fly? The pilot drives the fighter
to the takeoff spot. The controller tells
the pilot which way to go.

The pilot drives to the **runway**. The runway is a long, straight piece of land.

Let's roll! The fighter jet speeds down
the runway and takes off!

The pilot kicks in the **afterburners**.
They make the plane go even faster.

The pilot tucks in the landing gear. The fighter plane climbs high in the sky!

Fighter planes often fly in **formation**. The planes stay close together and look for the enemy.

These fighter planes need more **fuel**.
They will have to visit a tanker jet.

A tanker jet carries lots of fuel. It sends
fuel through a tube to the fighter jet.
The tube is called a **boom**.

This fighter plane is full of fuel. It is
ready for its next job.

We're lucky to have fighter planes
on our side.

Facts about Fighter Planes

- Fighter planes first fought in World War I.

- Fighters are numbered in the order they are invented. So an F-15 is an older type of plane than an F-16.

- The F-16 can fly up to 1,300 miles per hour. The F-15 goes up to 1,800 miles per hour. The speediest race car can only go about 200 miles per hour.

- Most fighter planes can fly about 50,000 feet in the air. Regular airplanes only fly as high as 30,000 feet.

- The U.S. Navy and U.S. Marine Corps fly F-14s and F/A-18s. These planes can take off and land on huge ships called aircraft carriers.

- An F-15 gets fuel about every 3,000 miles.

Parts of a Fighter Plane

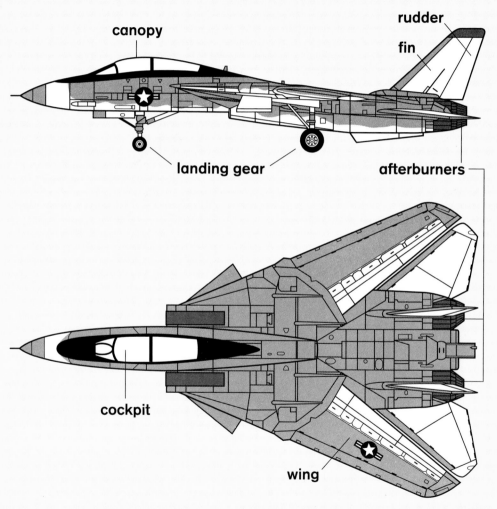

canopy

rudder

fin

landing gear

afterburners

cockpit

wing

Glossary

afterburners: parts of jet engines that give the plane extra speed

boom: a long tube that sends fuel from a tanker jet to a fighter plane in midair

canopy: the part that covers the pilot's area

cockpit: the place where the pilot sits

formation: a close grouping of fighter planes

fuel: liquid that keeps the jet engine running

jet engines: the part that powers the jet by pushing air through the engine very fast

runway: a long, straight piece of land that planes use to take off and land

Index

About the Author

Jeffrey Zuehlke has never flown a fighter plane, but he sure wishes he could. He loves to go to air shows and watch fighter planes roar across the skies above him.

Photo Acknowledgments

The photographs in this book appear courtesy of: United States Air Force, front cover, pp. 4, 5, 6, 8, 9, 10, 12, 13, 16, 17, 18, 19, 20, 23, 24, 25, 26, 27; United States Navy, pp. 3, 7, 11, 14, 15, 21, 22. Illustration on p. 29 © Laura Westlund/Lerner Publications Company.